Family Bike Ride

By Ann Staman

Illustrated by Tatjana Mai-Wyss

"Come on!"

said Dad.

"Come on!"

3

"Here I come!"

said Grandpa.

"Look at me!"

5

"Here I come!"

said Grandma.

"Here I come!"

Mom said,

"Here I come!

Look at me!"

9

"Look!"

said the brother.

"Look at me!"

11

"Here I come!"

said the sister.

"Look at me!"

"Here we come!"

said the twins.

"Look at us!"